FIX-IT and FORGET-IT® kids' Cookbook

Sweet Baked Oatmeal
Page 20

Chili

ity Punch
66

ccoli Casserole
Page 92

Page 105

Treat

Fix-It and Forget-It® kids' Cookbook

50 Favorite Recipes to Make in a Slow Cooker

Phyllis Pellman Good

Rebecca Good Fennimore, Photography Editor

Good Books

Intercourse, PA 17534
800/762-7171
www.GoodBooks.com

Acknowledgments

Rebecca Good Fennimore brought her love of food and cooking, and her experience as a sixth-grade teacher, to this project—helping to select recipes and to adapt them, and serving as a liaison with the food stylists and photographer. Thank you, Rebecca!

I am also grateful to Bonne di Tomo, one imaginative and diligent food stylist, along with her assistants, Sarah and Lisa.

Many thanks, too, to members of our staff who brainstormed and offered helpful ideas and even some cooking prep: Kate Good, Jan Mast, and Barb Carper.

Thank you, Sweet Infinity, for sharing some of your retro dishes and serving pieces.

Thank you, Jeremy Hess, for your professionalism and utter goodwill.

And Merle, whose idea I believe this book was in the first place, I don't have enough words to express my gratitude.

—*Phyllis Pellman Good*

All photography © 2010 by Jeremy Hess Photographers/JH
Design by Cliff Snyder

FIX-IT AND FORGET-IT® KIDS' COOKBOOK
Copyright © 2010 by Good Books, Intercourse, PA 17534

International Standard Book Number: 978-1-56148-704-2
Library of Congress Catalog Card Number: 2010021045

Library of Congress Cataloging-in-Publication Data

Good, Phyllis Pellman
  Fix-it and forget-it kids' cookbook : 50 favorite recipes to make in a slow cooker / Phyllis Pellman Good.
      p. cm.
  Includes index.
  ISBN 978-1-56148-704-2 (alk. paper)
  1. Electric cookery, Slow--Juvenile literature. 2. Quick and easy cookery--Juvenile literature. I. Title.
  TX827.G638 2010
  641.5'884--dc22   2010021045

Table of Contents

Fruity Waffle Topping
Page 22

The Simplest "Baked" Potatoes
Page 76

Chocolate Covered Pretzels
Page 122

Crunchy Snack Mix
Page 64

Big Juicy Burgers
Page 30

Welcome to the Kitchen— and This Cookbook!

Hey Kids—

Now you can make real meals! With the help of this fine bunch of recipes— and a slow cooker—you can fix breakfast, lunch, and dinner. Plus desserts and party food.

When you make food with a slow cooker, you have to think a little differently. Because the food takes longer to cook (remember—"slow" cooker), you will probably want to prepare a recipe the evening before you are going to serve and eat it.

In other words, if you decide to have Lip-Smacking Lasagna on Wednesday night, prepare the recipe on Tuesday night. Cook it during the day on Wednesday.

Or if it's summertime and you're at home during the day, prepare Tempting Tortilla Casserole early in the afternoon so it's ready by suppertime.

You can make a whole meal with this *Cookbook* if you have two or three slow cookers. Suggest that to your parents. They'll love your help in the kitchen. And now and then as you make these recipes, you'll need their help, too. You can be a team—the Real-Meal Cookers!

Happy Cooking—and Eating!

Phyllis Pellman Good

Tempting Tortilla Casserole
Page 82

To the Adults Who Are Cooking with Kids—

Take your children a step beyond nachos and cupcakes. Let them prepare a tasty main dish in that easy-to-get-along-with appliance—the slow cooker.

Perhaps your biggest job related to this Cookbook is helping the child plan ahead. Several hours separate the preparation of the dish from serving and eating it.

On weekends and during the summer, the child can fix the recipe in the morning or early afternoon for that evening's dinner. During the school year, the child will probably need to prepare the recipe the evening before the day of serving it.

A few other suggestions:

1 Be willing to yield your space to the child who is cooking. While a child should never be left alone to cook, be prepared to let the child occupy your kitchen as fully as necessary.

2 Try as much as possible to serve as a coach, rather than being in charge.

3 You'll need patience. Efficiency is not the highest value in this experience!

4 You'll need flexibility. Kids like to experiment with new ingredients and different procedures than given. Through it all, remember to be an encourager!

5 Realize that children enjoy the tactile experience of cooking. They're as interested in the process as they are in the final product.

6 Expect messes. Show the child how to clean them up—cheerfully!

7 Consider taking the child along grocery shopping. That will enlarge his/her understanding of the whole food process.

8 Cooking is a natural activity for kids. Allow your own sense of wonder to be renewed—along with the child's!

9 Invite the child to prepare a dish—or two—for a gathering of family or friends.

Cooking together is one friendly and engaging way to bring your children into the kitchen with you. When they help to fix a meal that they and their family enjoy, they'll be back to make more!

Learning to Know Your Slow Cooker

Slow Cookers Have Three Main Parts

1 The electrical unit. This is the outer part with the cord attached and the dial on the front.

2 The inner crock. This is the "bowl" that you put the food into.

3 The lid.

Learn Your Slow Cooker's Personality

Some slow cookers cook hot and fast. Others cook more slowly.

Most of the recipes in this book give you a range of cooking times. For example, "3-4 hours."

When you make a recipe for the first time, cook it for the shortest amount of time suggested in the recipe.

If the dish isn't quite finished at the end of that time, cook it for another 30-60 minutes, or until the dish is fully cooked.

When the recipe is cooked just the way you like it, write the length of cooking time that worked best in your cookbook. Yup. Write in your book. Then you'll know the right cooking time the next time you make the recipe.

Important Safety Alert!

When a slow cooker is turned on and cooking, all 3 parts get hot. Use potholders when touching or lifting any part of a slow cooker that's working.

A slow cooker stays hot for a while even after it's turned off. Keep your potholders handy.

How Full Should You Make Your Slow Cooker?

Slow cookers usually work best when they're 2/3 full.

Don't Lift the Lid...

...while your slow cooker is cooking!

When you lift the lid, heat escapes and slows down the cooking. If you just can't resist, add 15 minutes to the cooking time for each time you take off the lid to check how the food is doing.

A Big Question:
When should you turn on the slow cooker so the food is ready when you want to eat it?

Slow cookers are designed to cook food slowly, so you need to plan ahead to make sure your food is ready to eat on time.

1 First, check the Prep Time so you know how long it will take to **prepare** the recipe you want to make.

2 It's often easiest to prepare food for your slow cooker the day before you're going to eat it. Follow the recipe directions for preparation. Then, place the inner crock in the fridge. The next day, your food is all ready to cook in the slow cooker.

3 Next, check the Cooking Time so you know how long it will take to **cook** the recipe.

4 Then talk to your parent to figure out when to turn on your slow cooker.

5 If the recipe does not need to cook for more than a few hours, you can turn on your slow cooker when you get home from school.

6 If the recipe needs to cook for 8-10 hours, you can turn it on before you leave for school in the morning.

7 If the food needs to cook longer than a few hours, but not up to 8-10 hours, ask an adult to turn it on for you during the day while you're at school.

8 In the summer, during vacations, and on weekends, just make sure you plan ahead and allow enough time to slow-cook your recipe.

9 With a little bit of planning, it is easy to *Fix-It and Forget-It*!

Turning On Your Slow Cooker— 4 Easy Steps

1. Pop the inner crock into the electrical unit.
2. Put on the lid.
3. Plug in the electrical unit.
4. Switch on the dial to the right temperature setting.

Tasty Tomato Soup
Page 42

9

How to Follow a Slow Cooker Recipe

Cooking is great fun! Just follow the steps below to learn how to read a recipe, and you'll be ready to go.

1 Read the whole recipe from beginning to end before you start cooking.

2 Read the prep time and cooking time. Do you have enough time to complete the recipe?

3 Remember that a slow cooker can cook while you are not at home. It is often easiest to prepare the recipe the night before you're going to eat it. (In other words, do everything but cook the recipe in the slow cooker.) Then put your slow cooker crock in the refrigerator until it's time to turn it on the next day.

Gooey Chocolate Pudding Cake
Page 104

4 Read the Ingredient and Equipment Lists and get everything together that you need.

5 You will sometimes see "*divided*" after certain ingredients on a recipe's Ingredient List. In "Gooey Chocolate Pudding Cake" (page 104), "*divided*" comes after "1 cup sugar" on the Ingredient List. You'll need a <u>total</u> of 1 cup sugar. But you don't put it in all at once. In Step 2, you use ½ cup. In Step 3, you use the other ½ cup.

6 You will sometimes see "*optional*" after certain ingredients on a recipe's Ingredient List. In "Fruity Waffle Topping" (page 22), "*optional*" comes after "½ cup chopped walnuts" on the Ingredient List. You can decide whether or not you want to include walnuts.

7 Now start cooking!

Learning to Measure

To make a recipe turn out right, you have to measure right. And you need the right equipment.

Use glass measuring cups to measure liquids. These cups have lines on their sides so you know how high to fill them. Pour the liquid ingredient in slowly until it reaches the correct line on the glass measuring cup.

Use stacked measuring cups for dry ingredients. These cups come in sets with a different sized cup for each specific measurement—usually ¼, ⅓, ½, and 1 cup.

When you measure flour and sugar, hold the measuring cup over your container of flour and sugar. Fill your cup so that it is overflowing. Then run the back of a butter knife across the top of the cup so the extra dry ingredient falls back into its container. When you measure brown sugar, pat it down into the cup until it is level with the top. To measure cut-up foods, cut them first, and then place them in the measuring cup until they reach the top.

Use measuring spoons to measure small amounts of liquid or dry ingredients. You may need to level them off on the top with the back of a butter knife or the side of your finger.

To measure butter, look at the measuring marks on the wrapper around each stick so you can cut off the amount you need. The marks are usually measured in tablespoons. Use the Conversion Chart on this page if you need a different measurement.

Cooking Abbreviations

t. or tsp. = teaspoon
T. or Tbsp. = tablespoon
c. = cup
pt. = pint
qt. = quart
oz. = ounce
lb. = pound
pkg. = package

Conversion Chart

A pinch/dash = less than ⅛ teaspoon
1 tablespoon = 3 teaspoons
⅛ cup = 2 tablespoons
¼ cup = 4 tablespoons
⅓ cup = 5 tablespoons + 1 teaspoon
½ cup = 8 tablespoons
⅔ cup = 10 tablespoons + 2 teaspoons
¾ cup = 12 tablespoons
8 fluid ounces = 1 cup
1 pint = 2 cups
1 quart = 2 pints
1 quart = 4 cups
1 gallon = 4 quarts
16 ounces = 1 pound

Equipment List

Aluminum foil – A paper-thin sheet of metal used to cover food items.

Cheesecloth – A loosely woven fabric that you draw together to create a small bag to hold whole spices.

Colander – A bowl with holes in it used to drain water or other liquids from foods.

Cookie sheet – A flat metal sheet used for baking cookies.

Cooking spray –A liquid you spray on the inside of the inner crock so food won't stick.

Cutting board – A board that you chop or cut ingredients on.

Glass measuring cup – A glass cup, used to measure liquids, with measurements printed on its side.

Jar with a tight-fitting lid – Used to shake ingredients together until well mixed, such as salad dressings.

Kitchen shears – A type of scissors used to cut herbs and other food items.

Ladle – A long-handled dipper used for transferring liquid from one container to another.

Measuring cups – Cups in different sizes, used to measure dry ingredients.

Measuring spoons – Spoons in different sizes used to measure small amounts of liquid or dry ingredients.

Microwave-safe glass bowl – Cookware made of glass that is safe to use in the microwave. Metal items are not safe to use in a microwave.

Mixing bowls – Bowls of different sizes in which you mix ingredients together.

Plastic wrap – A sheet of plastic that covers food.

Potholders – Mittens or pads to hold hot pots, pans, lids, and baking sheets.

Rolling pin – A roller used to flatten an item such as dough for a piecrust.

Rubber spatula – A narrow flexible blade used for cleaning food out of containers.

Safety can opener – A tool to open cans that creates a safe, smooth edge around the opening.

Sealable plastic bag – A plastic bag that can be sealed tightly.

Shallow bowl – A bowl with short sides for dipping foods into.

Slotted spoon – A large spoon with holes in it so that liquid can drain out of it.

Safety Tips

1. Make sure an adult is always nearby when you're cooking. Ask for help when you have questions or if a container is too heavy or too hot to handle.
2. Wash your hands with warm, soapy water before you start cooking. Wash your hands right after working with raw meat or eggs.
3. Wear an apron.
4. Tie back your hair if it's long. ☺
5. Wear clothing without baggy sleeves.
6. Keep your slow cooker away from water. It is dangerous for electrical appliances to get wet. Also, dry your hands well before working with the slow cooker.
7. Use potholders to handle hot items.
8. Clean up any spills right away.
9. Have an adult help you when a recipe tells you to use a knife.
10. Use microwave-safe containers. Metal cannot be safely used in a microwave.
11. It's a good idea to put ingredients away when you're done using them.
12. When you are finished cooking, gather together all of the dirty dishes and utensils. Wipe the counter and work area. Wash the dirty dishes and help clean up the mess. (That will encourage your mom or dad to let you cook again! Plus it's part of cooking.)

Timer – A tool that keeps time as you cook.

Toothpick – Used to tell if cakes are done.

Twist tie – A short, paper-covered wire used to twist around a bag to close it.

Waxed paper – A sheet of paper that has a waxy coating so that food items won't stick to it.

Whisk – A utensil made of wire loops, used for mixing liquid ingredients together.

Wooden spoon – Used for mixing and stirring almost any kind of food.

Best Breakfasts

Blueberry Fancy

Makes 12 servings   •   Prep Time: 10-15 minutes   •   Cooking Time: 3-4 hours

If you like sweet treats, you'll love having this dish for breakfast. It's fun to make on the weekends as a brunch. You can also serve it as a dessert.

INGREDIENTS

1 loaf Italian bread

1 pint blueberries

8-oz. pkg. cream cheese

6 eggs

1½ cups milk

1 tsp. vanilla

EQUIPMENT

5-qt. slow cooker

Medium-sized mixing bowl

Whisk

Big spoon

1 Tear the bread into bite-sized pieces. Place half of the bread pieces into the slow cooker.

2 Drop half of the blueberries on top of the bread.

3 Have an adult help you cut the cream cheese into cubes, each about ½-inch square.

4 Sprinkle half of the cream cheese cubes over the blueberries.

5 Put the rest of the bread pieces on top of the cream cheese in the slow cooker.

6 Then layer the rest of the blueberries on top of the bread.

7 Finally, layer the rest of the cream cheese cubes on top of the blueberries.

8 Have an adult help you break the eggs into a medium-sized mixing bowl.

9 Add the milk and vanilla to the eggs and whisk them together until they are well mixed.

10 Carefully spoon or pour the egg mixture over the bread, blueberries, and cheese.

11 Cover your slow cooker. Cook on Low for 3-4 hours, until the dish is set. You will know that it is set if you move the slow cooker gently and the food does not move!

Serving Suggestion: *Serve with* **maple syrup** *or* **blueberry sauce** *drizzled over top.*

Hearty Ham and Cheese Breakfast Casserole

Makes 6 servings • Prep Time: 15 minutes • Cooking Time: 3-4 hours

This is a big, filling breakfast. Make it for an easy brunch with a side of fruit salad.

INGREDIENTS

8 slices bread

2 cups (8 oz.) grated cheddar, Swiss, *or* American, cheese

1 cup cooked, chopped ham

4 eggs

1 cup light cream, *or* milk

¼ tsp. salt

1 Tbsp. parsley

1 cup evaporated milk

a sprinkle of paprika

EQUIPMENT

Cooking spray

3- to 4-qt. slow cooker

Medium-sized mixing bowl

Safety can opener

Whisk

Potholder

Table Knife

1 Lightly grease the inside of your slow cooker with cooking spray.

2 Tear the crusts off each slice of bread. Then tear the bread into bite-sized squares. Put the torn bread (without the crusts) into the bottom of your slow cooker.

3 Sprinkle the grated cheese on top of the bread.

4 Then put the ham cubes on top of the cheese.

5 Have an adult help you crack the eggs into a medium-sized mixing bowl. Add the cream, salt, and parsley to the eggs.

6 Use a safety can opener to open the can of evaporated milk. Add 1 cup of evaporated milk to the egg mixture.

7 Whisk together the egg mixture until well mixed.

8 Carefully pour the egg mixture over the bread, cheese, and ham in the slow cooker.

9 Sprinkle the Casserole lightly with paprika.

10 Cover the slow cooker. Cook on Low for 3-4 hours.

11 After 3 hours, use a potholder to lift the lid. Stick a table knife into the center. If nothing is sticking to the knife, or if only fine crumbs are sticking to it, it is done. Otherwise, cover the slow cooker and cook for another hour.

19

Sweet Baked Oatmeal

Makes 4-6 servings • Prep Time: 10 minutes • Cooking Time: 2½-3 hours

This Baked Oatmeal is special. It's almost like having dessert for breakfast. But it's healthy, so your parents will be happy, too.

INGREDIENTS

⅓ cup vegetable oil

½ cup sugar

2 cups dry quick oatmeal

1½ tsp. baking powder

½ tsp. salt

¾ cup milk

1 large egg

EQUIPMENT

3-qt. slow cooker

Paper towel

Large wooden spoon

Small mixing bowl

Whisk

1 Carefully pour the oil into your slow cooker.

2 Use a paper towel to grease the bottom and sides of your slow cooker with the oil.

3 Add the sugar, oatmeal, baking powder, salt, and milk to your slow cooker. Mix well with a large wooden spoon.

4 Ask an adult to help you crack the egg into a small mixing bowl. Beat the egg with a whisk.

5 Carefully pour the egg into the oats mixture. Mix well.

6 Cover the slow cooker.

7 Bake the oatmeal on Low for 2½-3 hours.

Serving Suggestion: *Baked Oatmeal tastes great when topped with* **milk**. *You can also top it with other tasty ingredients such as* **craisins, brown sugar**, *or* **nuts**.

You can have fun with this Baked Oatmeal by adding different ingredients each time you make it. You can add ½ cup of your favorite chopped fruit or chocolate chips if you wish.

Fruity Waffle Topping

Makes 10-12 servings • Prep Time: 5 minutes • Cooking Time: 3 hours

This makes the perfect topping for waffles. It is also great over pancakes or as a dessert over cake or ice cream.

INGREDIENTS

1 qt. unsweetened applesauce

2 cups apple slices, peeled *or* unpeeled

1 pt. fresh *or* frozen blueberries

½ Tbsp. ground cinnamon

½ cup pure maple syrup

1 tsp. almond flavoring

½ cup chopped walnuts, *optional*

EQUIPMENT

Cooking spray

3½- to 4-qt. slow cooker

Large wooden spoon

Potholder

Ladle

1 Lightly spray the inside of your slow cooker with cooking spray.

2 Carefully stir together the applesauce, apple slices, and blueberries in the slow cooker.

3 Add cinnamon and maple syrup to the apple blueberry mixture. Mix well.

4 Cover the slow cooker and turn the heat to Low.

5 Cook the Fruity Topping on Low for 3 hours.

6 Just before you are ready to serve the Topping, use a potholder to remove the slow cooker lid.

7 Add the almond flavoring, and walnuts if you wish, to the Topping mixture. Stir carefully.

8 When you are ready to serve, use a ladle to carefully scoop the Topping onto fresh waffles, pancakes, cake, or ice cream.

You can buy sliced apples in the grocery store.

Cheesy Egg and Broccoli Casserole

Makes 6 servings • Prep Time: 10 minutes • Cooking Time: 3½-4 hours

This yummy breakfast is an easy way to enjoy eggs in the morning.

INGREDIENTS

24-oz. carton small-curd cottage cheese

10-oz. pkg. frozen chopped broccoli, thawed and drained

2 cups (8 oz.) shredded cheddar cheese

⅓ cup flour

3 Tbsp. finely chopped onion

½ tsp. salt

half a stick (¼ cup) butter

6 eggs

extra shredded cheese, *optional*

EQUIPMENT

Cooking spray

4-qt. slow cooker

Large mixing bowl

Large wooden spoon

Small microwave-safe glass bowl

Plastic wrap

Potholders

Medium-sized mixing bowl

Whisk

1 Lightly grease the inside of your slow cooker with cooking spray.

2 In a large mixing bowl, mix together the cottage cheese, thawed broccoli, 2 cups cheddar cheese, flour, chopped onion, and salt with a large wooden spoon.

3 Place the butter in a small microwave-safe glass bowl. Cover with plastic wrap. Microwave on High for 30 seconds, or until melted. Use potholders to remove the bowl.

5 Carefully pour the butter into the broccoli mixture.

6 Have an adult help you crack the eggs into a separate medium-sized mixing bowl. Whisk until well mixed. Carefully pour the eggs into the broccoli mixture. Mix well.

7 Spoon the broccoli mixture into your slow cooker. Cover. Cook on High for 1 hour.

8 Using a potholder, take off the lid and stir the broccoli mixture.

9 Once you've stirred the food, cover the slow cooker. Turn the heat to Low.

10 Cook 2½-3 hours on Low until the eggs are set. You will know that the Casserole is set if you move the slow cooker gently and the food does not move!

11 Sprinkle with extra shredded cheese, if you wish, and serve.

You can buy chopped onions in the grocery store.

Peanut Butter Granola

Makes 16-20 servings • Prep Time: 10 minutes • Cooking Time: 1½ hours • Cooling Time: 30-60 minutes

*This is a delicious breakfast cereal. If you take one bite,
you won't be able to stop eating it. It's also a great snack food.
Or, you can sprinkle it over some ice cream for a dessert.*

INGREDIENTS

6 cups dry oatmeal

½ cup wheat germ

½ cup toasted coconut

½ cup sunflower seeds

½ cup raisins

2 sticks (1 cup) butter

1 cup peanut butter

1 cup brown sugar

EQUIPMENT

Large wooden spoon

4- or 5-qt. slow cooker

Medium-sized microwave-
    safe glass bowl

Plastic wrap

Rubber spatula

Timer

Potholder

Greased cookie sheet

Waxed paper

Airtight container

1 Mix the oatmeal, wheat germ, coconut, sunflower seeds, and raisins together with a wooden spoon in a large slow cooker.

2 Place the butter, peanut butter, and brown sugar in a medium-sized microwave-safe glass bowl. Cover with plastic wrap.

3 Microwave on High for 1 minute, or until the mixture is melted.

4 Stir the butter mixture. Then, using a rubber spatula, carefully pour the butter mixture over the oatmeal mixture in the slow cooker. Mix well.

5 Cover the slow cooker. Cook on Low 1½ hours.

6 While the Granola is cooking, set the timer for 15 minutes. When the timer buzzes, stir the Granola. Use a potholder to remove the slow cooker lid. Stir the Granola and then cover the slow cooker.

7 Set the timer for 15 minutes again. Repeat Step 6 four more times.

8 When the Granola has cooked for a total of 1½ hours, ask an adult help you scoop the it onto a greased cookie sheet lined with waxed paper so that it can cool.

9 When the Granola is completely cool, break it into chunks and store it in an airtight container so it's ready to enjoy whenever you wish.

Love These Lunches

Big Juicy Burgers

Makes 8 servings • Prep Time: 15 minutes • Cooking Time: 7-9 hours

Hamburgers are everybody's favorite food. Now you can make your own Burgers! Don't forget to share them with your friends and family. They'll love when you cook!

INGREDIENTS

1 cup chopped onions

¼ cup chopped celery

2 lbs. ground beef

1 tsp. salt

½ tsp. pepper

2 cups tomato juice

2 tsp. minced garlic

1 Tbsp. ketchup

1 tsp. Italian seasoning

½ tsp. salt

EQUIPMENT

4- or 5-qt. slow cooker

Large mixing bowl

Medium-sized mixing bowl

You can buy chopped onions and celery in the grocery store. You can also buy minced garlic in the grocery store.

1 Place the chopped onions and celery in your slow cooker.

2 Place the beef, 1 tsp. salt, and pepper into a large mixing bowl. Use your hands to mix the salt and pepper into the beef. Divide the dough into eight balls, each the same size.

3 Flatten the eight balls of beef so they look like hamburger patties. Place the patties in the slow cooker on top of the onions and celery. Try not to stack them. If you have to, stagger them so they don't lie exactly on top of each other. Wash your hands well.

4 In a medium-sized mixing bowl stir together the tomato juice, minced garlic, ketchup, Italian seasoning and ½ tsp. salt. Pour this sauce over the patties in your slow cooker.

5 Cover your slow cooker. Cook the Burgers on Low for 7-9 hours.

Serving Suggestion: *To serve, place each Big Juicy Burger with a bit of the sauce on a **hamburger roll**. Feel free to add toppings of your choice: **cheese, pickles, lettuce, tomato** or **mustard** if you wish. Serve with **crackers, chips,** or **fries** if you wish.*

Fun Alphabet Soup

Makes 5-6 servings • Prep Time: 5 minutes • Cooking Time: 6½-8½ hours

This Alphabet Soup is easy to make and fun to eat. Pack it in your lunch for school and your friends will be impressed that you made it!

INGREDIENTS

½ lb. beef stewing meat, *or* round steak, cubed

14½-oz. can stewed tomatoes

8-oz. can tomato sauce

1 cup water

1 envelope dry onion soup mix

10-oz. pkg. frozen vegetables, partially thawed

½ cup uncooked alphabet noodles

EQUIPMENT

4-qt. slow cooker

Safety can opener

Potholders

1 Place the cubed meat in your slow cooker.

2 Use a safety can opener to open the stewed tomatoes and tomato sauce. Carefully pour them into your slow cooker. Stir well.

3 Add the water and soup mix to the tomato mixture in the slow cooker.

4 Cover your slow cooker. Cook the soup on Low for 6-8 hours, until the meat is tender but not dry. Ask an adult to help you check if the meat is done cooking after it has cooked for 6 hours.

5 Then turn your slow cooker heat to High.

6 Use a potholder to remove the lid. Stir in the vegetables and alphabet noodles.

7 Add more water if the soup looks too thick and dry.

8 Use a potholder to cover the slow cooker. Cook the soup on High for 30 minutes, or until the vegetables are cooked.

Serving Suggestion: *Serve with **crackers** if you wish.*

Chunky Chili

Makes 4-6 servings • Prep Time: 15 minutes • Cooking Time: 1½-2 hours

INGREDIENTS

1 lb. ground beef

16-oz. can kidney beans, undrained

15-oz. can black beans, undrained

14½-oz. can diced tomatoes, undrained

1 pkg. dry taco seasoning mix

half a 12-oz. jar salsa

pinch of sugar

EQUIPMENT

Large microwave-safe glass bowl

Wooden spoon

Plastic wrap

Potholders

Colander

Mixing bowl

4-qt. slow cooker

Safety can opener

1 Place the ground beef in a microwave-safe glass bowl. Stir the meat with a wooden spoon, breaking it into smaller pieces.

2 Cover the bowl with plastic wrap. Microwave on High for 2 minutes.

3 Use potholders to remove the bowl. Stir the meat to break up clumps.

4 Cover and return to the microwave. Cook on High for another 2 minutes.

5 Use potholders to remove the bowl. Stir the meat, making sure there are no pink spots. If you see pink, cover the bowl and microwave it on High for 1 minute and 30 seconds.

6 Use potholders to remove the bowl.

7 Set a colander over a mixing bowl. Ask an adult to help you spoon the meat into the colander so the liquid can drain into the bowl. (You won't need the liquid.)

8 Then carefully spoon the meat from the colander into the slow cooker.

9 Using a safety can opener, open the cans of kidney beans, black beans, and diced tomatoes. Pour the undrained beans and tomatoes into the slow cooker.

10 Add the taco seasoning, salsa, and pinch of sugar. Mix well.

11 Cover your slow cooker. Heat the Chili on High until it is boiling. You will know it is boiling when you see tiny bubbles on the top. When it is boiling, turn the heat to Low.

12 Let the Chili cook on Low for 1½ hours.

13 If you like a thicker Chili, use a potholder to remove the lid after 1½ hours. Let it cook a bit longer without the lid so that the Chili will thicken.

Serving Suggestion: *Top individual servings with your choice of **guacamole, sour cream, shredded cheese, sliced olives, fresh diced tomatoes, tortilla chips,** and **onions.***

Broccoli Corn Bread

Makes 8 servings • Prep Time: 10 minutes • Cooking Time: 6 hours

Who knew you could make Corn Bread in a slow cooker?
This bread is great to eat with Chunky Chili.

INGREDIENTS

4 eggs

1 stick (½ cup) butter

10-oz. pkg. frozen chopped broccoli, thawed

1 cup chopped onions

1 box corn bread mix

1 cup (8 oz.) cottage cheese

1¼ tsp. salt

EQUIPMENT

Large mixing bowl

Whisk

Small microwave-safe glass bowl

Plastic wrap

Potholders

Rubber spatula

Wooden spoon

3- to 4-qt. slow cooker

Cooking spray

Toothpick

1 Ask an adult to help you crack 4 eggs into a large mixing bowl. Use a whisk to beat the eggs well.

2 Place butter in a small microwave-safe glass bowl. Cover the bowl with plastic wrap.

3 Put the bowl in the microwave on High for 30 seconds, or until the butter is melted.

4 Use potholders to remove the bowl. Using a rubber spatula, carefully scrape the butter into the mixing bowl with the eggs.

5 Add the chopped broccoli, chopped onion, corn bread mix, cottage cheese, and salt to the mixing bowl. Stir well with a wooden spoon.

You can buy chopped onions in the grocery store.

6 Grease the inside of your slow cooker with cooking spray. Spoon or pour the Corn Bread mixture into the slow cooker.

7 Cover your slow cooker. Cook the Corn Bread on Low for 6 hours.

8 After 6 hours, use a potholder to remove the lid. Stick a toothpick into the center of the Bread and pull it out. If the toothpick looks wet, the Bread needs to continue cooking. If it has some dry crumbs on it, it's finished cooking.

Serving Suggestion: *To serve, you can scoop the Bread out of your slow cooker. Or, you can ask an adult to help you flip the slow cooker upside down until the Bread comes out. Then ask an adult to help you cut it into wedges.*

Ham and Potato Chowder

Makes 5 servings • Prep Time: 15 minutes • Cooking Time: 8 hours

This chunky soup makes a great lunch any time of the year.

INGREDIENTS

1 cup chopped celery

⅓ cup chopped onions

¼ lb. cooked ham

5-oz. pkg. scalloped potatoes

sauce mix from potato pkg.

4 cups chicken broth

salt to taste

pepper to taste

2 cups half-and-half

⅓ cup flour

EQUIPMENT

4-qt. slow cooker

Kitchen shears

Large wooden spoon

Small mixing bowl

Whisk

Potholder

Timer

1 Place chopped celery and onions in your slow cooker.

2 Using a kitchen shears, carefully cut ham into thin strips. Add ham to slow cooker.

3 Add potatoes, sauce mix, chicken broth, salt, and pepper to your slow cooker. Stir together gently until everything is well mixed.

4 Cover your slow cooker. Cook the Chowder on Low heat for 7 hours.

5 In a small mixing bowl, whisk together the half-and-half and flour.

6 After 7 hours of cooking time, use a potholder to remove your slow cooker lid. Carefully pour the half-and-half and flour mixture into the slow cooker. Mix well.

7 Cover your slow cooker. Continue to cook the Chowder on Low for up to 1 hour. During this hour, set the timer for 15 minutes. Stir the Chowder. Repeat this 3 more times—or until the Chowder gets thick. Use your potholder any time you touch the lid.

Serving Suggestion: *Serve with **crackers** if you wish.*

You can buy chopped onions and celery in the grocery store.

Easy Taco Filling

Makes 4-6 servings • Prep Time: 20 minutes • Cooking Time: 6-8 hours

INGREDIENTS

1 lb. ground beef

1 cup chopped onions

2 15-oz. cans chili beans, undrained

15-oz. can Santa Fe, *or* Mexican, *or* Fiesta, corn, undrained

¾ cup water

¼ tsp. cayenne pepper, *optional*

½ tsp. garlic powder, *optional*

EQUIPMENT

Microwave-safe glass bowl

Wooden spoon

Plastic wrap

Potholders

Colander

Large mixing bowl

4-qt. slow cooker

Safety can opener

1 Place the ground beef in a microwave-safe glass bowl. Stir the meat with a wooden spoon, breaking it into smaller pieces. Stir the onions into the meat.

2 Cover the bowl with plastic wrap. Microwave on High for 2 minutes.

3 Use potholders to remove the bowl. Stir the meat mixture to break up clumps.

4 Cover and return to the microwave. Cook on High for another 2 minutes.

5 Use potholders to remove the bowl. Stir the meat, making sure there are no pink spots. If you see pink, cover the bowl and microwave it on High for 1 minute and 30 seconds.

6 Use potholders to remove the bowl.

7 Set a colander over a mixing bowl. Ask an adult to help you spoon the meat into the colander so the liquid can drain into the bowl. (You won't need the liquid.)

8 Spoon the meat and onions from the colander into the slow cooker.

9 Use a safety can opener to open the cans of beans and corn. Pour them into the meat mixture in the slow cooker. Add water, and seasonings if you wish, to the slow cooker. Mix well.

You may add more or less than ¾ cup water, depending on how your slow cooker cooks — and how soupy you like your tacos to be.

10 Cover your slow cooker. Cook the Taco Filling on Low for 6-8 hours.

Serving Suggestions: *Serve the Taco Filling in warmed* **soft corn tortillas** *or* **hard taco shells.** *Or, serve as a dip with* **plain corn tortilla chips.** *Top your taco with any of the following ingredients:* **shredded cheese, sour cream, diced tomatoes, sliced olives, shredded lettuce, guacamole,** *or* **salsa.**

Tasty Tomato Soup

Makes 6 servings • Prep Time: 15-20 minutes • Cooking Time: 5-8 hours

You will love making this yummy Soup for lunch. It tastes even better when you eat it with a grilled cheese sandwich.

INGREDIENTS

1 sprig celery leaves

half an onion

46-oz. can tomato juice

8-oz. can tomato sauce

½ cup water

1 Tbsp. bouillon granules

½ tsp. dried basil

2 Tbsp. sugar

1 bay leaf

½ tsp. whole cloves

EQUIPMENT

4-qt. slow cooker

Cooking spray

Kitchen shears

Safety can opener

Cheesecloth

Twist tie

Large spoon

Potholder

Slotted spoon

1 Grease the inside of your slow cooker with cooking spray.

2 Wash the celery well. Use a kitchen shears to carefully snip the sprig of celery leaves into bite-sized pieces. Add the celery to the greased slow cooker.

3 Ask an adult to help you thinly slice the onion. Add the onion to the slow cooker.

4 Use a safety can opener to open the cans of tomato juice and tomato sauce. Pour them into the slow cooker.

5 Add the water, bouillon granules, basil, sugar, and bay leaf to the tomato mixture.

6 Lay the cheesecloth on the counter. Pile the cloves in the middle of it. Gather up the sides of the cloth and twist them together at the top so the cheesecloth is closed tightly. Tie a twist tie around it to hold it tight.

7 Add the cheesecloth "bag" to the slow cooker. Stir gently until everything is mixed together well.

8 Cover your slow cooker. Cook the Soup on Low for 5-8 hours.

9 Use a potholder to remove the lid from the slow cooker. Use a slotted spoon to fish out the bay leaf and the cloves in the cheesecloth. Throw them away.

If you prefer a thicker soup, add ¼ cup instant potato flakes to the end of Step 9. Stir well and cook 5 minutes longer.

Serving Suggestion: *Serve with **crackers** if you wish.*

Heaping Hot Dog Sandwiches

Makes 5-8 servings • Prep Time: 20 minutes • Cooking Time: 1¾ hours

These fun Sandwiches are great for a picnic. If you like hot dogs, you'll love this recipe!

INGREDIENTS

10¾-oz. can cheddar cheese soup

¼ cup finely chopped onions

2 Tbsp. sweet pickle relish

1 tsp. prepared mustard

1 lb. hot dogs

½ cup sour cream

EQUIPMENT

Safety can opener

Rubber spatula

3-qt. slow cooker

Wooden spoon

Kitchen shears

Potholder

1 Use a safety can opener to open the can of soup. Use a rubber spatula to scrape the soup into your slow cooker.

2 Add the onions, relish, and mustard to the soup in your slow cooker. Mix well with a wooden spoon.

3 Use a kitchen shears to carefully slice the hot dogs into about ½-inch slices. Mix the slices into the cheesy sauce.

4 Cover your slow cooker. Cook on Low for 1¾ hours.

5 Ten minutes before the end of the cooking time, use a potholder to carefully remove the lid of the slow cooker.

6 Stir in the sour cream. Cover the slow cooker for the last ten minutes of cooking time.

Serving Suggestion: *Serve in* **hot dog buns** *or over squares of hot* **corn bread**.

You can buy chopped onions in the grocery store.

Chicken Noodle Soup

Makes 6-8 servings • Prep Time: 15 minutes • Cooking Time: 3½-8½ hours

Chicken Noodle Soup is so comforting. Now you can make this Soup yourself!

INGREDIENTS

10¾-oz. can cream of chicken soup

10¾-oz. can cream of mushroom soup

5 cups water

2 small cans chopped cooked chicken

10-oz. pkg. frozen mixed vegetables, thawed

¼ tsp. pepper

1½ cups dry egg noodles

EQUIPMENT

Safety can opener

Rubber spatula

4-qt. slow cooker

Wooden spoon

Potholder

You may use chicken broth in place of all, or part of, the water.

1 Use a safety can opener to open the cans of soup. Use a rubber spatula to scrape the soup into your slow cooker.

2 Carefully pour the water into your slow cooker. Stir gently with a wooden spoon until the soups and water are blended together well.

3 Use a safety can opener to open the cans of chicken. Add to the soup mixture in the slow cooker.

4 Stir the vegetables and pepper into the slow cooker.

5 Cover your slow cooker. Cook on Low for 6-8 hours, or on High for 3-4 hours.

6 If you cook the Soup on Low heat, turn the slow cooker to High heat after it's cooked for 6-8 hours.

7 Use a potholder to remove the lid. Stir the noodles into the soup mixture.

8 Cover the slow cooker and cook the Soup on High for 20-30 minutes, or until the noodles just finish cooking. Ask an adult help you test if the noodles are done cooking.

You may substitute other flavors of cream soups. Or you can use two cans of cream of chicken soup and skip the can of cream of mushroom soup.

The Best Beef Barbecue

Makes 10 servings • Prep Time: 15 minutes • Cooking Time: 2½ hours

These meaty sandwiches are fun to eat during an outdoor picnic in the summertime.

INGREDIENTS

2 lbs. ground beef

¾ cup chopped onions

2 Tbsp. Worcestershire sauce

1½ cups ketchup

4 Tbsp. brown sugar

1 cup water

EQUIPMENT

Microwave-safe glass bowl

Wooden spoon

Plastic wrap

Potholders

Colander

Mixing bowl

4-qt. slow cooker

1 Place the ground beef in a microwave-safe glass bowl. Stir the meat with a wooden spoon, breaking it into smaller pieces. Stir the onions into the meat.

2 Cover the bowl with plastic wrap. Microwave on High for 2 minutes.

3 Use potholders to remove the bowl. Stir the meat mixture to break up clumps.

4 Cover and return to the microwave. Cook on High for another 2 minutes.

5 Use potholders to remove the bowl. Stir the meat, making sure there are no pink spots. If you see pink, cover the bowl and microwave it on High for 1 minute and 30 seconds.

6 Use potholders to remove the bowl.

7 Set a colander over a mixing bowl. Ask an adult to help you spoon the meat into the colander so the liquid can drain into the bowl. (You won't need the liquid).

8 Then carefully spoon the meat mixture from the colander into the slow cooker.

9 Add the Worcestershire sauce, ketchup, brown sugar, and water to the meat mixture in the slow cooker. Mix well.

10 Cover your slow cooker. Cook on Low for 2½ hours.

Serving Suggestion: *Pile the Beef Barbecue into **sandwich rolls**. Serve with **French fries** if you wish.*

You can buy chopped onions in the grocery store.

Snackin' Time

Mini Hot Dogs and Meatballs

Makes 8 servings • Prep Time: 5 minutes • Cooking Time: 2-3 hours

*This is a great treat when you are having friends over.
It is also easy to make for an after-school snack.*

INGREDIENTS

18 frozen cooked Italian
 meatballs (½-oz. each)

8-oz. pkg. miniature hot dogs, *or*
 little smoked sausages

1½ cups meatless spaghetti
 sauce

1 cup bottled barbecue sauce

1 cup bottled chili sauce

EQUIPMENT

3- or 4-qt. slow cooker

Large mixing spoon

1 Put all of the ingredients
into your slow cooker
and mix them with a large
spoon.

2 Once everything is
mixed well, cover the
slow cooker and turn
it to High.

3 Cook on High for 2 hours, or on Low for 3
hours, until the food is hot. Before turning the slow
cooker off, ask an adult to test if the food is hot
enough to eat.

*If you like pepperoni,
you can choose to
add a 3½-oz. pkg.
of sliced pepperoni to
Step 1.*

Pizza Dip

Makes 4-6 servings • Prep Time: 15 minutes • Cooking Time: 1 hour

If you love pizza, you'll love this yummy snack. You'll enjoy making it for your family or friends.

INGREDIENTS

19-oz. can Italian-style stewed tomatoes with juice

4 cups grated cheddar cheese

2 cups grated mozzarella cheese

loaf of Italian bread, sliced

EQUIPMENT

3½-qt. slow cooker

Cooking spray

Safety can opener

Large spoon

Rubber spatula

Potholder

Toaster oven

Serving bowl

The Dip will stay creamy on Low heat for up to 4 hours. It tastes best if you eat it right away.

1 Lightly spray the inside of your slow cooker with cooking spray.

2 Use a safety can opener to open the can of stewed tomatoes. Do not drain them. Carefully pour the entire can of tomatoes into the lightly greased slow cooker.

3 Stir the cheddar cheese and mozzarella cheese into the tomatoes in the slow cooker.

Feel free to add ¼ lb. thinly sliced pepperoni to Step 3.

4 Cover the slow cooker and cook on High for 45-60 minutes, or until the cheese melts.

5 You may need to stir the food occasionally and scrape down the sides of the slow cooker with a rubber spatula so that the food doesn't burn. Use a potholder to carefully lift the lid.

6 Toast the bread slices. Let them cool. When they are cool, tear them into bite-sized pieces. Try to keep a crust on each piece so you can hold onto it while you dunk the bread in the Dip. Place the bread pieces in a serving bowl.

7 After the Dip has cooked for 45-60 minutes, turn the slow cooker to Low.

8 Serve the Pizza Dip with the toasted bread bites.

You can use a different type of bread, other than Italian.

Minty Hot Chocolate

Makes 6 servings • Prep Time: 5 minutes • Cooking Time: 2-3 hours

Hot Chocolate is everyone's favorite drink in the winter.
This yummy treat has chocolate-covered mint candies in it, too!

INGREDIENTS

6 small chocolate-covered
   cream-filled mint patties

5 cups milk

½ cup chocolate malted milk
   powder

1 tsp. vanilla

EQUIPMENT

2- to 3-qt. slow cooker

Large wooden spoon

Potholders

1 In your slow cooker, use a wooden spoon to mix the chocolate-covered mint patties with the milk, malted milk powder, and vanilla.

2 Cover your slow cooker. Heat the Hot Chocolate on Low for 2-3 hours.

3 After 1 hour, use a potholder to take off the lid. Stir the drink gently to help melt the mint patties. Then cover your slow cooker.

5 After 1 more hour, stir the drink again to make sure the mint patties have melted.

6 Serve hot.

Serving Suggestion: *Have an adult help you use an immersion blender or hand-held mixer to beat the drink until it is frothy. Top each cup with* **whipped cream** *if you wish.*

Cheesy Broccoli Dip

Makes 24 servings • Prep Time: 20 minutes • Cooking Time: 1 hour

Broccoli and cheese are always a good combo.
Enjoy this snack any time of the year.

INGREDIENTS

Half a red bell pepper

2 cups frozen chopped broccoli, thawed

2 8-oz. containers Ranch dip

½ cup grated Parmesan cheese

2 cups shredded cheddar cheese

EQUIPMENT

Kitchen shears

2-qt. slow cooker

Large wooden spoon

1 Using a kitchen shears, carefully chop the red bell pepper into enough little chunks to fill ¼ cup. Place the pieces in your slow cooker.

2 Add all of the other ingredients to the red bell pepper in the slow cooker. Mix the Dip together with a large wooden spoon.

3 Cover. Cook the Dip on Low for 1 hour.

Serving Suggestion: *Serve with **pita chips, veggie chips,** or **raw, cut-up vegetables**.*

You may use Swiss cheese, or any other cheese that you like, instead of the cheddar cheese.

Red Hot Apple Cider

Makes 16 1-cup servings • Prep Time: 2 minutes • Cooking Time: 1½-2 hours

This hot drink is fun for Valentine's Day. It also warms you up when it's snowing.

INGREDIENTS

1 gallon apple cider *or* apple juice

1¼ cups cinnamon candy hearts

EQUIPMENT

5-qt. slow cooker

Large wooden spoon

1 Mix the cider and the cinnamon hearts together in your slow cooker with a large wooden spoon.

2 Cover the slow cooker. Cook the Cider on Low for 1½-2 hours, or until the hearts melt, and it's as hot as you like it.

Serving Suggestion: *When you are ready to enjoy your drink, put a **4-inch-long cinnamon stick** into each cup. This drink tastes best when it's hot.*

Hot Sweet Caramel Dip

Makes 3 cups of Dip   •   Prep Time: 5 minutes   •   Cooking Time: 15 minutes

This sweet treat is fun to make with friends for a sleepover or a party.

INGREDIENTS

1 stick (½ cup) butter

½ cup light corn syrup

1 cup brown sugar

12-oz. can sweetened condensed milk

apple slices, *or other cut-up fruit, or* small cookies

EQUIPMENT

Microwave-safe glass bowl

Safety can opener

Mixing spoon

Plastic wrap

Potholders

Rubber spatula

3-qt. slow cooker

1 Place the butter in a microwave-safe glass bowl.

2 Add the corn syrup and brown sugar to the bowl.

3 Use a safety can opener to open the can of sweetened condensed milk.

4 Pour the milk into the bowl with the rest of the Dip mixture. Mix the Dip well.

Add ½ cup peanut butter to the Dip in Step 2 if you wish.

5 Cover with plastic wrap. Place the glass bowl into the microwave.

6 Microwave on High for 2 minutes, or until the Dip is boiling. You will see little bubbles at the top of the Dip when it is boiling. Use potholders to remove the bowl.

7 Using a rubber spatula, scrape the Dip mixture into your slow cooker.

8 Cover the slow cooker. Cook on Low for 15 minutes, or until it is warm. Have an adult help you test if it is warm enough to eat.

9 When you are ready to eat, carefully dip your fresh apple slices, or other cut-up fruit, or cookies into the hot caramel.

You can buy sliced apples in the grocery store.

Crunchy Snack Mix

Makes 3 quarts Snack Mix   •   Prep Time: 5 minutes   •   Cooking Time: 3 hours

INGREDIENTS

3 cups thin pretzel sticks

4 cups Wheat Chex

4 cups Cheerios

12-oz. can salted peanuts

half a stick (¼ cup) butter

1 tsp. garlic powder

1 tsp. celery salt

½ tsp. seasoned salt

2 Tbsp. grated Parmesan cheese

EQUIPMENT

Large mixing bowl

Large wooden spoon

Small microwave-safe glass bowl

Plastic wrap

Potholder

4-qt. slow cooker

Timer

Tightly covered container

If you are allergic to peanuts, you can simply replace the 12-oz. can of peanuts with 2 cups of either pretzels or cereal.

1 Mix pretzels, Wheat Chex, Cheerios and peanuts in a large bowl with a wooden spoon.

2 Place butter into a small microwave-safe glass bowl. Cover with plastic wrap. Microwave the butter on Low for 30 seconds, or until it is melted. Using a potholder, remove the bowl.

If you like Corn Chex, you can add 3 cups of Corn Chex to the mix. Then use 3 cups of Wheat Chex (instead of 4 cups) and 3 cups of Cheerios (instead of 4 cups).

3 Stir the garlic powder, celery salt, seasoned salt, and Parmesan cheese into the butter.

4 Carefully pour the butter mixture over the pretzels and cereal.

5 Stir until everything is well mixed.

6 Spoon the Mix into your slow cooker. Cover. Cook on Low for 2½ hours.

7 You will need to stir the Mix every 30 minutes. Use a timer to remind yourself. Use a potholder to lift the lid. Carefully stir the Mix with a wooden spoon. Cover while it continues to cook.

8 After 2½ hours, use your potholder to take off the lid.

9 Let the Mix cook without the lid for another 30 minutes on Low.

10 Serve warm or at room temperature.

11 After the Mix has cooled, store it in a tightly covered container.

Hot Fruity Punch

Makes 10 1-cup servings • Prep Time: 10 minutes • Cooking Time: 1 hour

This drink will warm you up when it's cold outside. You can serve it with a dessert for a special occasion, such as Mother's Day.

INGREDIENTS

1 qt. cranberry juice

3 cups water

6-oz. can frozen orange juice concentrate, thawed

10-oz. pkg. frozen red raspberries, thawed

2 oranges, sliced

6 sticks cinnamon

12 whole allspice

EQUIPMENT

4-qt. slow cooker

Large wooden spoon

Cheesecloth, about 6 inches square

Twist tie

1 Mix the cranberry juice, water, thawed orange juice concentrate, and thawed raspberries together with a large wooden spoon in your slow cooker.

2 Have an adult help you carefully slice the oranges. Place the sliced oranges in the slow cooker with the Punch mixture.

3 Lay the piece of cheesecloth on the counter. Lay the cinnamon sticks and allspice on top of it. Bring all 4 corners of the cloth together to make a little bag with the spices inside. Twist the ends of the cheesecloth together tightly. Close it with the twist tie. Place the cheesecloth bag in the slow cooker with the Punch mixture.

4 Cover your slow cooker. Heat the Punch on High for 1 hour, or until it's really hot. Have an adult help you check to see if the Punch is hot.

5 Turn the heat to Low when you are ready to serve the punch.

Super Bowl Dip

Makes 15 servings • Prep Time: 15 minutes • Cooking Time: 1-2 hours

INGREDIENTS

1 lb. ground beef

½ lb. Velveeta cheese

half an envelope dry
  taco seasoning mix

half a 24-oz. jar salsa

half a 16-oz. can
  refried beans

EQUIPMENT

Microwave-safe glass
  bowl

Wooden spoon

Plastic wrap

Potholders

Colander

Mixing bowl

3- to 4-qt. slow cooker

Safety can opener

1 Place the ground beef in a microwave-safe glass bowl. Stir the meat with a wooden spoon, breaking it into smaller pieces.

2 Cover the bowl with plastic wrap. Microwave on High for 2 minutes.

3 Use potholders to remove the bowl. Stir the meat to break up clumps.

4 Cover and return to the microwave. Cook on High for another 2 minutes.

5 Use potholders to remove the bowl. Stir the meat, making sure there are no pink spots. If you see pink, cover the bowl and microwave it on High for 1 minute and 30 seconds.

6 Use potholders to remove the bowl.

7 Set a colander over a mixing bowl. Ask an adult to help you spoon the meat into the colander so the liquid can drain into the bowl. (You won't need the liquid.)

8 Then carefully spoon the meat from the colander into the slow cooker.

9 Using your hands, break the Velveeta cheese apart into cubes.

10 Stir the taco seasoning mix, salsa, and cheese into the meat in the slow cooker.

11 Use a safety can opener to open the can of refried beans. Stir the beans into the meat.

12 Cover the slow cooker. Cook the Dip on Low for 1-2 hours, or until the cheese melts.

13 Stir the Dip before you serve it.

Serving Suggestion: *Serve with your favorite* **tortilla chips,** **bread cubes,** *or* **pretzels.** *Top with* **cherry tomatoes** *and* **olives,** *too, if you wish.*

Doing Dinner

Super Spaghetti Sauce

Makes 6-8 servings • Prep Time: 30 minutes • Cooking Time: 7 hours

Spaghetti is a fun meal to have with friends.

INGREDIENTS

1 lb. ground beef

1 cup chopped onions

2 14-oz. cans diced tomatoes, with juice, undrained

6-oz. can tomato paste

8-oz. can tomato sauce

1 bay leaf

2 tsp. minced garlic

2 tsp. dried oregano

1 tsp. salt

2 tsp. dried basil

1 Tbsp. brown sugar

½ tsp. dried thyme

EQUIPMENT

Microwave-safe glass bowl

Wooden spoon

Plastic wrap

Potholders

Colander

Mixing bowl

4-qt. slow cooker

Safety can opener

Rubber spatula

Slotted spoon

1 Place the ground beef in a microwave-safe glass bowl. Stir the meat with a wooden spoon, breaking it into smaller pieces. Stir the onions into the meat.

2 Cover the bowl with plastic wrap. Microwave on High for 2 minutes. Use potholders to remove the bowl. Stir the meat to break up clumps. Cover. Microwave on High for another 2 minutes.

3 Use potholders to remove the bowl. Stir the meat, making sure there are no pink spots. If you see pink, cover the bowl and microwave it on High for 1 minute and 30 seconds.

4 Use potholders to remove the bowl. Set a colander over a mixing bowl. Ask an adult to help you spoon the meat into the colander so the liquid can drain into the bowl. (You won't need the liquid.)

5 Then spoon the meat and onion mixture from the colander into the slow cooker.

6 Use a safety can opener to open the diced tomatoes, tomato paste and tomato sauce. Use a rubber spatula to scrape them into the slow cooker.

7 Add the bay leaf, minced garlic, oregano, salt, basil, brown sugar, and thyme to the slow cooker. Mix well.

8 Cover your slow cooker. Cook the Sauce on Low for 7 hours. Use a slotted spoon to fish out the bay leaf before serving

9 If the sauce is runny, use your potholder to remove the lid for the last hour of cooking.

Serving Suggestion: *Serve over* **spaghetti** *or other* **pasta** *of your choice. Sprinkle with some grated* **Parmesan cheese** *if you wish.*

Creamy Lasagna

Makes 8-10 servings • Prep Time: 15 minutes • Cooking Time: 5-6 hours

Your family will fall in love with this creamy lasagna. They will think you worked really hard to make something so delicious.

INGREDIENTS

3 eggs

2 cups (16 oz.) evaporated milk

3 cups (24 oz.) cottage cheese

1 tsp. salt

½ tsp. pepper

1 cup (8 oz.) sour cream

2 cups cubed cooked ham

7 uncooked lasagna noodles

EQUIPMENT

Large mixing bowl

Safety can opener

Large wooden spoon

4- or 5-qt. slow cooker

1 Have an adult help you crack 3 eggs into a large mixing bowl.

2 Use a safety can opener to open the cans of evaporated milk. Add the 2 cups of evaporated milk to the eggs in the mixing bowl.

3 Add the cottage cheese, salt, pepper, sour cream, and cubed cooked ham to the mixing bowl. Stir well with a large wooden spoon.

4 Place ⅓ of the creamy ham mixture into the bottom of your slow cooker.

5 Layer half the uncooked noodles on top of the ham mixture. Break them if you need to to make them fit.

6 Repeat Step 4, using half the remaining creamy mixture.

7 Repeat Step 5, using all the remaining noodles.

8 Cover the noodles with the remaining creamy ham sauce. Make sure that the noodles are not sticking out of the sauce. Push them down in so they're fully covered.

9 Cover your slow cooker. Cook on Low for 5-6 hours.

Serving Suggestion: *Serve with a **green salad** or **vegetable** if you wish.*

The Simplest "Baked" Potatoes

Makes 4-12 servings (or 1 big potato for each person)   •   Prep Time: 5 minutes
Cooking Time: 4-10 hours (depending on how many potatoes you've put into the cooker;
the more potatoes, the longer it takes them to cook)

What makes these "baked" potatoes so cool are the yummy toppings. Throw a party and ask each person to bring a different topping. Then let people choose to top their potatoes with whatever they wish.

INGREDIENTS

4-12 baking potatoes

EQUIPMENT

Fork

Aluminum foil

3½- to 5-qt. slow cooker

Potholder

1 Prick each potato all over—at about 6 different places—with a fork.

2 Wrap each potato in a square of aluminum foil.

3 Place the potatoes in your slow cooker. Do not add water. Cover your slow cooker.

4 Cook the potatoes on High for 4-5 hours, or on Low for 8-10 hours, or until the potatoes are soft when your prick them with a fork. (If you're cooking on High, check the potatoes after they've cooked for 4 hours. If you're cooking on Low, check after 8 hours.)

5 To test if the potatoes are done, use a potholder to remove your slow cooker lid. Then, with your potholder still on, carefully unwrap one of the potatoes. Prick it with a fork.

6 If it feels soft, the potatoes are done. If it still feels hard, carefully rewrap the potato and cook it for another 30-60 minutes, or until it is soft when you prick it again with a fork.

Serving Suggestion: *Top your baked potato with* **cooked broccoli pieces, shredded cheese, sour cream, crispy pieces of bacon,** *or whatever you wish.*

Yummy Italian Meatloaf

Makes 8-10 servings • Prep Time: 15 minutes • Cooking Time: 8 hours

You can really impress your family by making them this scrumptious dinner. If you have any leftovers, you can take a slice of meatloaf, or make a meatloaf sandwich, for your lunch the next day.

INGREDIENTS

2 eggs

2 lbs. ground beef

⅔ cup dry quick-cooking oatmeal

1 envelope dry onion soup mix

½ cup pasta sauce (your favorite)

1 tsp. garlic powder

onion slices, *optional*

EQUIPMENT

Large mixing bowl

Whisk

4- to 5-qt. slow cooker

1 Ask an adult to help you crack 2 eggs into a large mixing bowl.

2 Use a whisk to beat the eggs well.

3 Add the ground beef, oatmeal, soup mix, pasta sauce, and garlic powder to the eggs in the mixing bowl.

4 Use your hands to mix all of the ingredients together well. Then form the meat into a big loaf, like a loaf of bread.

5 Carefully place the meat in your slow cooker. Wash your hands well.

6 If you like onions, ask an adult to help you slice an onion.

7 Place the onion slices on top of the Meatloaf.

8 Cover your slow cooker. Cook the Meatloaf on Low heat for 8 hours.

Serving Suggestion: *Serve the Meatloaf with **pasta**, topped with more of the **pasta sauce** that you mixed into the Meatloaf.*

Mac and Cheese

Makes 4-5 servings • Prep Time: 5 minutes • Cooking Time: 3 hours

This fun favorite is good as a whole meal for dinner or as a side dish. It's so simple to make. You will want to make it again and again.

INGREDIENTS

¼ stick (2 Tbsp.) butter

1½ cups uncooked macaroni

1 qt. milk

3 cups grated sharp cheddar cheese, *or* cubed Velveeta cheese

½ tsp. salt

¼ tsp. pepper

EQUIPMENT

Small microwave-safe glass bowl

Plastic wrap

Potholders

Rubber spatula

3-qt. slow cooker

1 Place the butter in a small microwave-safe glass bowl. Cover with plastic wrap.

2 Microwave the butter on High for 30 seconds, or until it is melted.

3 Use potholders to remove the bowl. Use a rubber spatula to scrape the butter into your slow cooker.

4 Add the macaroni, milk, cheese, salt, and pepper to the butter in your slow cooker. Stir well.

5 Cover your slow cooker. Cook the Mac and Cheese on Low for 3 hours.

Serving Suggestion: *This is also a special meal for lunch. Serve with a side of **veggies** and **yogurt** if you wish.*

81

Tempting Tortilla Casserole

Makes 4 servings • Prep Time: 20 minutes • Cooking Time: 4 hours

INGREDIENTS

1 lb. ground beef

1 envelope dry taco seasoning

16-oz. can fat-free refried beans

1½ cups (6 oz.) grated cheese of your choice, divided

bag of tortilla chips (for topping the Casserole)

EQUIPMENT

Cooking spray

3-qt. slow cooker

Microwave-safe glass bowl

Wooden spoon

Plastic wrap

Potholders

Colander

Mixing bowl

Safety can opener

Rubber spatula

1 Spray the inside of your slow cooker with cooking spray.

2 Place the ground beef in a microwave-safe glass bowl. Stir the meat with a wooden spoon, breaking it into smaller pieces.

3 Cover the bowl with plastic wrap. Microwave on High for 2 minutes. Use potholders to remove the bowl. Stir the meat to break up clumps. Cover. Microwave on High for another 2 minutes.

4 Use potholders to remove the bowl. Stir the meat, making sure there are no pink spots. If you see pink, cover the bowl and microwave it on High for 1 minute and 30 seconds.

5 Use potholders to remove the bowl. Set a colander over a mixing bowl. Ask an adult to help you spoon the meat into the colander so the liquid can drain into the bowl. (You won't need the liquid.)

6 Then spoon the meat from the colander into the slow cooker. Add the taco seasoning and mix well.

7 Sprinkle 1 cup of cheese over top of the meat.

8 Use a safety can opener to open the can of refried beans. Use a rubber spatula to scrape the beans on top of the cheese. Spread the beans out in an even layer. Be careful not to disturb the grated cheese while you do it.

9 Sprinkle the remaining cheese on top of the beans.

10 Cover your slow cooker. Cook on Low for 3-4 hours.

11 Top the Casserole with tortilla chips just before serving.

Serving Suggestion: *You may also add* **guacamole, sour cream,** *and diced* **tomatoes** *as toppings if you wish.*

Cheesy Green Beans

Makes 5-6 servings • Prep Time: 10 minutes • Cooking Time: 5-6 hours

This side dish goes well with lots of meals. You can also make it for a holiday meal to help your family at a really busy time.

INGREDIENTS

½ lb. Velveeta cheese

1 lb. frozen green beans

¼ cup chopped onions

¼ cup milk

1½ tsp. flour

EQUIPMENT

4-qt. slow cooker

Wooden spoon

Jar with a tight-fitting lid

1 Using your hands, break the Velveeta cheese apart into cubes.

2 Place the cheese, beans, and onions in your slow cooker. Mix well with a wooden spoon.

3 Place milk first, and then flour, in a jar with a tight-fitting lid. Shake them together until you don't see any flour lumps.

4 Stir the flour-milk mixture into the other ingredients in the slow cooker.

5 Cover your slow cooker. Cook on Low for 5-6 hours, or until the beans are fully cooked and heated through. Have an adult help you check if the beans are done.

Serving Suggestion: *Top with **French fried onions** if you wish.*

You can buy chopped onions in the grocery store.

Pizza in a Bowl

Makes 6 servings • Prep Time: 10 minutes • Cooking Time: 5-6 hours

This pasta dish is a cross between pasta and pizza. What could be better? Surprise your family with this delicious dish. Serve it for your next party and your friends will love it!

INGREDIENTS

14½-oz. can low-sodium diced tomatoes

26-oz. jar fat-free, low-sodium marinara sauce

4 oz. pepperoni, diced, *or* sliced

1 cup chopped bell peppers

1 cup chopped onions

1 cup water

1 Tbsp. Italian seasoning

1 cup uncooked macaroni

1½ cups fresh mushrooms, sliced, *optional*

1½ cups shredded mozzarella cheese

EQUIPMENT

Safety can opener

3½-qt. slow cooker

Potholder

1 Use a safety can opener to open the can of diced tomatoes. Pour the tomatoes into your slow cooker.

2 Add the marinara sauce, pepperoni, chopped peppers and onions, water, Italian seasoning, dry macaroni, and mushrooms if you wish.

3 Cover your slow cooker. Cook the pasta mixture on Low for 5-6 hours.

4 After the pasta has cooked, use a potholder to take the lid off of your slow cooker.

5 Carefully spoon the hot pasta mixture into bowls.

6 Sprinkle each with mozzarella cheese.

You can buy chopped bell peppers and onions in the grocery store.

Tasty Tuna Noodle Casserole

Makes 5-6 servings • Prep Time: 10 minutes • Cooking Time: 2-6 hours

This comforting Casserole will make you smile, no matter what kind of day you've had.

INGREDIENTS

2½ cups uncooked noodles

½ tsp. salt

½ cup finely chopped onions

½ cup shredded Swiss, *or* sharp cheddar cheese

¼ cup sliced almonds, *optional*

½ cup sliced mushrooms, *optional*

6- or 12-oz. can tuna, depending on how much you like tuna

10¾-oz. can cream of mushroom soup

half a soup can of water

1 cup frozen peas

EQUIPMENT

3-qt. slow cooker

Wooden spoon

Safety can opener

Rubber spatula

Timer

Potholder

1 Mix the uncooked noodles, salt, onions, cheese, and almonds and mushrooms if you wish, in your slow cooker with a large wooden spoon.

2 Use a safety can opener to open the cans of tuna and cream of mushroom soup. Use a rubber spatula to carefully scrape them into the slow cooker. Stir together gently.

3 Then fill up half of the empty soup can with water. Add the water to the tuna mixture.

4 Gently stir again until everything is well mixed.

5 Cover your slow cooker. Cook on High for 2-3 hours, or on Low for 4-6 hours.

6 You will need to stir the Casserole every hour or so. Set the timer to remind yourself. Make sure to use a potholder to take off the lid.

7 Twenty minutes before the end of the cooking time, use your potholder to remove the slow cooker lid. Stir in the peas. If you cooked the Casserole on High heat, turn it to Low heat at this point.

8 Cook the Casserole for 20 more minutes, and then it's time to eat!

You can buy chopped onions in the grocery store.

Party Meatball Subs

Makes 15 servings • Prep Time: 15 minutes • Cooking Time: 8-10 hours

These fun sandwiches will be the winner at your next party. Serve them with some chips and lemonade for a complete meal. Your friends won't be able to get enough of these subs!

INGREDIENTS

1 medium onion

half a 10-lb. bag prepared meatballs

26-oz. jar spaghetti sauce (your favorite flavor)

½ tsp. minced garlic

1 cup sliced mushrooms, *optional*

EQUIPMENT

7-qt. slow cooker

Large spoon

Timer

Potholder

1 Have an adult help you slice the onion. Place the sliced onion in your slow cooker.

2 Add the meatballs, jar of spaghetti sauce, minced garlic, and mushrooms if you wish to your slow cooker.

3 Mix well, stirring up from the very bottom so that the meatballs are covered in the sauce.

You can buy minced garlic in the grocery store.

4 Cover your slow cooker. Cook on Low for 8-10 hours.

5 You will need to stir the Meatballs every two hours or so. Set the timer to remind yourself.

6 Remember to use the potholder to remove the lid.

Serving Suggestion: *Serve in **hot dog buns** or **hoagie rolls**. Sprinkle grated **mozzarella cheese** over top of each filled roll if you wish.*

Crunchy Broccoli Casserole

Makes 4 servings • Prep Time: 10 minutes • Cooking Time: 2-4 hours

This side dish has a fun surprise on top. Potato Chips add some extra crunch!

INGREDIENTS

2 10-oz. pkgs. frozen chopped broccoli, thawed

1½ cups grated cheddar cheese, *divided*

¼ cup onions, finely chopped

10¾-oz. can cream of celery soup

1 cup baked potato chips, crushed

EQUIPMENT

4-qt. slow cooker

Cooking spray

Safety can opener

Rubber spatula

Wooden spoon

Small bowl

Potholder

1 Grease the inside of your slow cooker with cooking spray.

2 Place thawed broccoli, 1 cup of cheese, and onions in your slow cooker.

3 Use a safety can opener to open the can of soup. Use a rubber spatula to scrape the soup into your slow cooker. Mix everything together well with a wooden spoon.

4 Cover your slow cooker. Cook on Low for 3-4 hours, or on High for 2 hours.

5 Mix the remaining ½ cup of cheese and crushed potato chips together in a small bowl.

6 Thirty minutes before your cooking time is up, use a potholder to remove the lid. Sprinkle the potato chip and cheese mixture on top of the Casserole.

7 Do not put the lid back on the slow cooker or the chips will get soggy. Let the Casserole cook uncovered for its final 30 minutes.

You can buy chopped onions in the grocery store.

Italian Chicken Nuggets

Makes 4 servings • Prep Time: 5 minutes • Cooking Time: 1 hour

This is a quick dinner you can whip up after school. If no one else in your family has time to make dinner, you can make them this meal. It also tastes great as a lunch.

INGREDIENTS

13½-oz. pkg. frozen chicken nuggets

⅓ cup grated Parmesan cheese

28-oz. jar spaghetti sauce

4 oz. shredded mozzarella cheese

1 tsp. Italian seasoning

EQUIPMENT

3-qt. slow cooker

1 Place the nuggets in the bottom of your slow cooker. Try not to stack them, but if you have to, stagger them so they don't sit exactly on top of each other.

2 Sprinkle the nuggets with Parmesan cheese. Lift up any nuggets that are covering others and sprinkle the bottom ones with cheese, too.

3 Then layer in spaghetti sauce, mozzarella cheese, and Italian seasoning.

4 Cover your slow cooker. Cook on High for 1 hour, or until the chicken is tender but not dry or mushy. Ask an adult to help you check the chicken to see that the chicken is fully cooked.

Serving Suggestion: *Serve with a side **salad**.*

Lip-Smacking Lasagna

Makes 6-8 servings • Prep Time: 30-45 minutes • Cooking Time: 4 hours

INGREDIENTS

1 lb. ground beef

29-oz. can tomato sauce
(get a spicy variety if
you like spicy)

8-oz. pkg. lasagna
noodles, uncooked

4 cups shredded
mozzarella cheese

1½ cups (12 oz.) cottage
cheese

EQUIPMENT

6-qt. slow cooker

Cooking spray

Microwave-safe glass
bowl

Wooden spoon

Plastic wrap

Potholders

Colander

3 mixing bowls

Safety can opener

1 Spray the inside of your slow cooker with cooking spray.

2 Place the ground beef in a microwave-safe glass bowl. Stir the meat with a wooden spoon, breaking it into smaller pieces.

3 Cover the bowl with plastic wrap. Microwave on High for 2 minutes. Use potholders to remove the bowl. Stir the meat to break up clumps. Cover. Microwave on High for another 2 minutes.

4 Use potholders to remove the bowl. Stir the meat, making sure there are no pink spots. If you see pink, cover the bowl and microwave it on High for 1 minute and 30 seconds.

5 Use potholders to remove the bowl. Set a colander over a mixing bowl. Ask an adult to help you spoon the meat into the colander so the liquid can drain into the bowl. (You won't need the liquid.)

6 Then spoon the meat from the colander into a clean mixing bowl.

7 Use a safety can opener to open the can of tomato sauce. Pour the sauce into the meat in your mixing bowl. Mix well.

8 Spread one-fourth of the meat sauce on the bottom of your slow cooker.

9 Then layer one-third of the uncooked noodles over the sauce. (You may want to break them up so they fit better.)

10 Mix the two cheeses in a bowl. Spoon one-third of the cheeses over the noodles.

11 Repeat these layers twice, starting with the meat, then the noodles, then the cheese.

12 After you've completed three layers, put the rest of the sauce on top of the cheese.

13 Cover your slow cooker. Cook the Lasagna on Low for 4 hours.

Creamy Corn Pudding

Makes 3-4 servings • Prep Time: 15-20 minutes • Cooking Time: 4 hours

This corn is the perfect side dish for any family gathering. You can put your special touch on the meal by making this recipe.

INGREDIENTS

2 eggs

2 Tbsp. butter

16-oz. can cream-style corn

2 Tbsp. sugar

1 tsp. salt

⅛ tsp. pepper

2 Tbsp. flour

½ cup milk

EQUIPMENT

Large mixing bowl

Whisk

Small microwave-safe glass bowl

Plastic wrap

Potholder

Rubber spatula

Safety can opener

3-qt. slow cooker

1 Have an adult help you crack 2 eggs into a large mixing bowl. Mix the eggs well with a whisk.

2 Place the butter in a small microwave-safe glass bowl. Cover with plastic wrap.

3 Microwave for 30 seconds, or until the butter is melted.

4 Use a potholder to remove the bowl from the microwave. Use a rubber spatula to scrape the butter into the eggs.

5 Use a safety can opener to open the can of corn. Use a rubber spatula to scrape the corn into the egg and butter mixture.

6 Add the sugar, salt, pepper, flour, and milk to the mixing bowl. Mix well with the whisk.

7 Pour or spoon the corn mixture into your slow cooker.

8 Cover your slow cooker. Cook on Low for 4 hours.

Add ½ cup grated cheese to Step 6, if you wish.

Crunchy Chicken

Makes 8 servings • Prep Time: 15 minutes • Cooking Time: 3½-4 hours

This chicken gets its crunch from cereal. It's really fun to make and it tastes great, too! Serve it with the Cheesy Green Beans for a complete meal. Or pack it in your lunch box on a school day.

INGREDIENTS

3½ lbs. chicken legs and thighs, *or* whole chicken, cut up

3 eggs

5 cups rice, *or* corn, cereal

1 tsp. salt

½ tsp. black pepper

EQUIPMENT

Shallow mixing bowl

Sealed plastic bag

Rolling pin

6-qt. slow cooker

1 Have an adult help you remove the skin from the chicken pieces. Wash your hands thoroughly when you're finished.

2 Have an adult help you crack the eggs into a shallow mixing bowl.

3 Put the cereal in a sealed plastic bag. Roll the bag lightly with a rolling pin to crush the cereal.

4 One by one, dip each piece of chicken into the egg mixture.

5 One by one, place each piece of chicken into the bag with cereal. Seal the bag tightly. Shake well until the chicken is thoroughly coated with the cereal.

6 As you finish with each piece, place it into your slow cooker. Sprinkle the pieces with salt and pepper.

7 Cover your slow cooker. Cook on High for 3½-4 hours, or until the chicken is tender. Ask an adult to help you check the chicken to make sure it is fully cooked.

Can't Wait for Dessert

Gooey Chocolate Pudding Cake

Makes 8 servings • Prep Time: 15 minutes • Cooking Time: 2-3 hours

This gooey, sweet, chocolatey dessert will become one of your favorites. It tastes really great when you serve it with vanilla ice cream. This is fun for a birthday or whenever you want a sweet treat.

INGREDIENTS

1 cup dry all-purpose baking mix

1 cup sugar, *divided*

3 Tbsp. unsweetened cocoa powder, plus ⅓ cup, *divided*

½ cup milk

1 tsp. vanilla

1⅔ cups hot water

EQUIPMENT

3½-qt. slow cooker

Cooking spray

Medium-sized mixing bowl

Small mixing bowl

Wooden spoon

Potholder

Toothpick

The batter will rise to the top and turn into the Cake. Underneath will be a rich chocolate pudding. Make sure you scoop down to get some of the gooey chocolate when you serve the cake.

1 Spray the inside of your slow cooker with cooking spray.

2 In a medium-sized mixing bowl, mix together the baking mix, ½ cup sugar, 3 Tbsp. cocoa powder, milk, and vanilla. Spoon the batter into your slow cooker and spread it out evenly.

3 In a small mixing bowl, mix the remaining ½ cup sugar, ⅓ cup cocoa powder, and the hot water together. Carefully pour this mixture over the batter. Do not stir.

4 Cover your slow cooker. Cook the Cake on High for 2-3 hours.

5 After 2 hours, use a potholder to remove the lid. Carefully stick a toothpick into the center of the Cake and pull it out. If the toothpick looks wet, the Cake needs to keep cooking. If it has some dry crumbs on it, it's time to eat.

6 If the Cake needs to cook longer, continue to test it with a toothpick every 15 minutes until it's done.

Serving Suggestion: *Serve warm with* **vanilla ice cream.** *Top with* **powdered sugar** *and* **whipped cream** *if you wish.*

Tapioca Treat

Makes 10-12 servings   •   Prep Time: 15 minutes
Cooking Time: 3 hours and 20 minutes   •   Chilling Time: 3 hours or so

This cold pudding will be a hit with your friends.
You can add different fruit to the pudding if you wish.

INGREDIENTS

2 quarts milk

1 cup small pearl tapioca

1-1½ cups sugar

4 eggs

1 tsp. vanilla

1 cup grapes

1 cup crushed pineapple

1 cup frozen whipped topping, thawed, *or* whipped cream from a can

EQUIPMENT

4- or 5-qt. slow cooker

Whisk

Mixing bowl

Potholder

Ladle

Rubber spatula

Kitchen shears

Safety can opener

Big spoon

1 Mix the milk, tapioca, and sugar in your slow cooker with a whisk.

2 Cover your slow cooker. Cook the Tapioca on High for 3 hours.

3 Have an adult help you crack the eggs into a mixing bowl. Beat them well with a whisk. Add the vanilla to the eggs.

4 Use a potholder to remove the lid. Use a ladle to scoop out a little of the hot milk from the slow cooker. Carefully add the hot milk to the egg mixture. Stir the hot milk into the eggs well.

5 Then add the egg mixture to the slow cooker. Use a rubber spatula to scrape the bowl.

6 Cover your slow cooker. Cook the Tapioca on High for 20 more minutes.

7 Chill the tapioca completely. This may take 3 hours or so.

8 While it's chilling, use a kitchen shears to cut the grapes in half.

9 Use a safety can opener to open the crushed pineapple. Drain off the juice.

10 After the Tapioca has chilled completely, stir in the grapes, pineapple, and whipped topping or cream. Serve cold.

Crunchy Apple Crisp

Makes 6-8 servings • Prep Time: 10 minutes • Cooking Time: 2-3 hours

This warm dessert tastes yummy in the fall when apples are fresh and the weather is starting to turn cool. It's also a nice treat to make for a holiday meal.

INGREDIENTS

1 qt. canned apple pie filling

¾ cup dry quick oatmeal

½ cup brown sugar

½ cup flour

half a stick (¼ cup) butter, at room temperature

EQUIPMENT

Safety can opener

Rubber spatula

2- or 3-qt. slow cooker

Medium-sized mixing bowl

Wooden spoon

Kitchen Shears

Fork

1 Use a safety can opener to open the apple pie filling.

2 With a rubber spatula, carefully scrape the filling into your slow cooker.

3 In a medium-sized mixing bowl, mix together the dry oatmeal, brown sugar, and flour with a wooden spoon.

4 Using a kitchen shears, cut the butter into about 4 chunks. Drop the chunks into the dry oatmeal mixture in the mixing bowl. Use a fork to break up the butter and to mix it into the dry mixture until it gets crumbly.

5 Sprinkle the crumb topping over the apple filling. Do not mix it into the apple filling.

6 Cover your slow cooker. Cook the Crisp on Low for 2-3 hours.

Serving Suggestion: *This is best served warm with* **vanilla ice cream**. *Top with* **blueberries**, *other* **fruit**, *or* **nuts**, *if you wish.*

Haystacks

Makes 3 dozen pieces • Prep Time: 15 minutes
Cooking Time: 15 minutes • Cooling Time: 30 minutes

These candy treats get their name from their haystack shape. They are fun to take in your lunch or to make with friends after school.

INGREDIENTS

2 6-oz. pkgs. butterscotch chips

¾ cup chopped almonds

5-oz. can chow mein noodles

EQUIPMENT

2-qt. slow cooker

Wooden spoon

Waxed paper

Spoon

Covered container

1 Turn your slow cooker heat to High.

2 Place the butterscotch chips in your slow cooker.

3 Using a wooden spoon, stir the chips every few minutes until they're melted.

4 When the chips are completely melted, gently stir in the chopped almonds and the chow mein noodles.

5 When the Haystacks are well mixed, roll out a sheet of waxed paper.

6 Carefully scoop a spoon into the Haystack mixture and drop one spoonful of the Haystack mixture onto the waxed paper.

7 Continue to scoop Haystacks onto the waxed paper until the slow cooker is empty. Leave about an inch of space between each of the Haystacks.

8 Keep the Haystacks on the waxed paper until they are set. You can speed things up by placing them in the fridge until they're set.

9 Serve, or store in a covered container, placing waxed paper between the layers of candy so they don't stick together. Keep in a cool, dry place.

Cherry Cobbler

Makes 6-8 servings • Prep Time: 10 minutes • Cooking Time: 2½-5½ hours

This fruity dessert is good any time of the year. It tastes like a pie and a cake at the same time. It not only tastes delicious, it's also easy to make.

INGREDIENTS

16-oz. can cherry pie filling

1 egg

3 Tbsp. evaporated milk

1¾ cups dry cake mix of your choice

½ tsp. cinnamon

EQUIPMENT

3-qt. slow cooker

Cooking spray

Safety can opener

Rubber spatula

Medium-sized mixing bowl

Measuring spoon

Large wooden spoon

Potholder

Toothpick

1 Lightly spray the inside of your slow cooker with cooking spray.

2 Use a safety can opener to open the cherry pie filling. Use a rubber spatula to scrape the pie filling into the slow cooker.

3 Cover your slow cooker. Cook on High heat for 30 minutes.

4 While the pie filling is cooking, ask an adult to help you crack an egg into a medium-sized mixing bowl.

5 Use a safety can opener to open the can of evaporated milk. Measure the evaporated milk out and add it to the egg in the mixing bowl.

6 Add the cake mix and cinnamon to the egg mixture. Mix with a wooden spoon until the mixture is crumbly.

7 Using a potholder, remove the lid from the slow cooker. Then spoon the cake mixture on top of the hot pie filling. Do not stir it down into the cherries.

8 Use a potholder to cover the slow cooker. Turn the heat to Low and cook for 2-5 hours.

9 After 2 hours, use a potholder to remove the lid. Stick a toothpick into the center of the cake topping and pull it out. If the toothpick looks wet, the Cobbler needs to keep cooking. If it has some dry crumbs on it, it's finished cooking.

10 If the Cobbler needs to cook longer, test it with a toothpick every 15 minutes until it's done.

11 Allow to cool until the Cobbler is no longer hot. Serve warm or cooled.

Pumpkin Pie Pudding

Makes 4 6 servings • Prep Time: 15 minutes • Cooking Time: 6-7 hours

You can impress your family by making this dish for your Thanksgiving meal.

INGREDIENTS

2 eggs

15-oz. can solid pack pumpkin

12-oz. can evaporated milk

¼ stick (2 Tbsp.) butter

¾ cup sugar

½ cup buttermilk baking mix

1 Tbsp. pumpkin pie spice

2 tsp. vanilla

EQUIPMENT

Large mixing bowl

Whisk

Safety can opener

Rubber spatula

Small microwave-safe glass bowl

Plastic wrap

Potholders

Wooden spoon

4-qt. slow cooker

1 Ask an adult to help you crack 2 eggs into a large mixing bowl. Whisk the eggs until the yolks are broken and they are pale yellow.

2 Use a safety can opener to open the can of pumpkin and the can of evaporated milk.

3 Use a rubber spatula to scrape the pumpkin and evaporated milk into the large mixing bowl with the eggs.

4 Place the butter in a small microwave-safe glass bowl. Cover with plastic wrap.

5 Microwave on High for 30 seconds, or until the butter is melted. Use potholders to remove the bowl. Carefully pour the butter into the pumpkin mixture.

6 Add the sugar, baking mix, pumpkin pie spice, and vanilla to the pumpkin mixture. Use a wooden spoon to mix well.

7 Carefully spoon or pour the pumpkin mixture into your slow cooker.

8 Cover your slow cooker. Cook on Low heat for 6-7 hours, or until it's set. You will know that it is set if you move the slow cooker gently and the food does not move.

9 Let the Pudding cool before serving it. Eat it warm or at room-temperature.

Serving Suggestion: *Top with* **whipped cream.**

Chocolate Treats

Makes 2½-3 cups • Prep Time: 5 minutes • Cooking Time: 2½ hours

This is a perfect treat for a party!

INGREDIENTS

1 stick (½ cup) butter

1½ cups sugar

¼ cup whipping cream

6 1-oz. squares unsweetened chocolate

EQUIPMENT

Small microwave-safe glass bowl

Plastic wrap

Potholders

Rubber spatula

Wooden spoon

2-qt. slow cooker

Potholder

As long as you keep at least an inch of the chocolate in your slow cooker, you can keep the slow cooker turned on Low for up to 6 hours. Just make sure you stir it every 30 minutes or so.

1 Place the butter in a small microwave-safe glass bowl.

2 Cover the bowl with plastic wrap. Microwave the butter on High for 30 seconds, or until it is melted.

3 Use potholders to remove the bowl. Using a rubber spatula, carefully scrape the melted butter into your slow cooker.

4 Add the sugar to the slow cooker and use a wooden spoon to mix them together well.

5 Stir the whipping cream into the butter-sugar mixture in the slow cooker until it is well blended. Stir in squares of chocolate.

6 Cover your slow cooker. Cook on High for 30 minutes.

7 Using a potholder, remove the lid. Stir the chocolate mixture well.

8 Turn the slow cooker to Low. Cook the chocolate on Low for 2 hours.

Serving Suggestion: *Dip the following goodies into the warm chocolate:* **angel food** *or* **pound cake***, cut into bite-sized pieces;* **marshmallows***;* **apple slices***;* **banana chunks***;* **strawberries***; or a* **candy** *of your choice.*

Caramel Apples on Sticks

Makes 8-10 servings • Prep Time: 30 minutes • Cooking Time: 1-1½ hours

This recipe is so fun to make! Grab some friends and make it a party. You can find apples in the grocery store all year long, but this recipe is especially yummy in the fall.

INGREDIENTS

2 14-oz. bags of caramels

¼ cup water

8-10 medium apples, unpeeled

¼ cup, *or more if you need it,* granulated sugar

EQUIPMENT

Large wooden spoon

2-qt. slow cooker

Timer

Small shallow bowl

Waxed paper

Cooking spray

12 sturdy sticks (plus a few extras in case they break)

Rubber spatula

1 Unwrap all the caramels. Using a large wooden spoon, mix the caramels and water together in your slow cooker.

2 Cover the slow cooker. Cook the caramel mixture on High for 1-1½ hours, stirring every 5 minutes. You should probably set a timer so you don't forget!

3 While the caramels are melting, wash and dry the apples.

4 Pour the sugar into a small shallow bowl.

5 Spread a large piece of waxed paper, about 15 inches square, on the counter. Lightly grease it with cooking spray.

6 When the caramels have finished cooking, take a stick and carefully push it into an apple at the stem end.

7 Turn the slow cooker heat to Low. Carefully dip the apple into the hot caramel, turning the apple so that it is completely covered in caramel.

8 With help from an adult, hold the apple above the slow cooker and use a rubber spatula to scrape any extra caramel off the bottom of the apple.

9 Then dip the bottom of the caramel apple in the sugar. Doing this helps to keep it from sticking to the waxed paper. Place the apple on the greased waxed paper to cool.

10 Repeat Steps 6-9 with each of the other apples.

Fruit-Filled Cake
(also known as Dump Cake!)

Makes 8-10 servings • Prep Time: 15 minutes • Cooking Time: 2-3 hours

This cake is sometimes called Dump Cake because you just dump the ingredients in the slow cooker to make it. It's so simple and so yummy, too.

INGREDIENTS

21-oz. can blueberry *or* cherry pie filling

20-oz. can crushed pineapple

18½-oz. pkg. yellow cake mix

cinnamon

1 stick (½ cup) butter, straight out of the refrigerator

1 cup chopped nuts, *optional*

EQUIPMENT

Cooking spray

4-qt. slow cooker

Safety can opener

Rubber spatula

Kitchen shears

Potholders

Toothpick

Use a package of spice cake mix and a can of apple pie filling instead of yellow cake mix and blueberry, or cherry, pie filling.

1 Grease the inside, bottom, and sides of your slow cooker with cooking spray.

2 Use a safety can opener to open the blueberry, or cherry, pie filling and the crushed pineapple. Using a rubber spatula, scrape the pie filling into the greased slow cooker.

3 Scrape the crushed pineapple on top of the pie filling. Be careful not to mix the layers.

4 Sprinkle the dry cake mix on top of the pineapple. Do not mix the layers. Sprinkle the top of the cake mix with cinnamon.

5 Using a kitchen shears, carefully snip the butter into small pieces. Sprinkle these pieces on top of the cinnamon-covered cake mix.

6 Top the Cake with nuts if you wish. Do not stir!

7 Cover your slow cooker. Cook on High for 2-3 hours.

8 After 2 hours, use a potholder to remove the slow cooker lid. Carefully stick a toothpick into the center of the cake topping and pull it out. If the toothpick looks wet, the Cake needs to keep cooking. If it has some dry crumbs on it, it's finished cooking.

9 If the Cake needs to cook longer, test it with a toothpick every 15 minutes until it's done.

10 Let the Cake cool until it's either warm or room temperature. Then it's ready to eat.

Serving Suggestion: *Serve with **vanilla ice cream**.*

Chocolate Covered Pretzels

Makes 10-12 servings • Prep Time: 30 minutes • Cooking Time: 15-30 minutes

This dessert is perfect for your next party. It is also a great gift for your friends, family, or teachers. Put a few pretzels in a bag and tie it with a colorful bow.

INGREDIENTS

8 oz. milk, *or* dark, chocolate coating wafers

1 bag mini pretzels

1 bag pretzel rods

4 oz. white chocolate coating wafers, *optional*

your favorite assorted sprinkles, *optional*

EQUIPMENT

1-qt. slow cooker

Wooden spoons

Waxed paper

Small microwave-safe bowl

Sealed plastic bag

Scissors

1 Place milk, or dark, chocolate coating wafers in your slow cooker. Turn heat to Low.

2 Using a wooden spoon, stir the chocolate occasionally until it is melted. Then turn off your slow cooker.

3 Dip each pretzel into the chocolate and carefully coat ¾ of each pretzel with the chocolate. (You can skip coating the part where you hold onto the pretzel.)

4 As you finish dipping each pretzel, lay it on a sheet of waxed paper to cool completely.

5 If you like white chocolate, place it in a small microwave-safe bowl. Microwave on High for 1 minute. Stir.

6 Microwave on High for 1 more minute. Stir.

7 Microwave on High for 30 seconds more at a time, but just until the chocolate is smooth when you stir it. (If it gets too hot it will burn.)

8 Carefully spoon the white chocolate into a sealed plastic bag. Cut off the corner of the bag to make a small hole.

9 Squeeze the melted white chocolate out of that hole, drizzling it over the chocolate-covered pretzels. See what designs you can make!

10 Top with your favorite sprinkles if you wish.

11 Let the pretzels cool completely before eating them or putting them in bags.

Glossary

Beat – Stir fast with a spoon, fork, whisk, or electric mixer in order to make a mixture smooth.

Boiling – Cook a liquid to such a hot temperature that big bubbles appear.

Broken yolks –The result of whisking an egg yolk so that it is no longer whole. The yellow center becomes runny.

Chopped – Food that is cut into small pieces.

Coat – Completely covering the surface of a food with another food.

Cover – Put a lid or sheet of foil, waxed paper, or plastic wrap over food.

Crack eggs – Tap the egg on the side of a bowl. Then, working over a bowl, pull the eggshell halves apart and let the egg white and yolk fall into the bowl. (Do not let the shell fall into the bowl!)

Diced – Chop food into small, square, even-sized pieces.

Divided – Separate individual ingredients into smaller batches.

Drain – Pour off a liquid in which a food has been cooked or stored.

Grease – Rub the inner crock of a slow cooker with butter or oil, or spray it with cooking spray, so that food cooked in it won't stick.

Layer – Stack one food item on top of another.

Melt – Heat something solid until it becomes a liquid.

Minced – Cut food into very small pieces.

Mix – Stir ingredients with a spoon, fork, whisk, or mixer until smooth or well blended.

Prick – Lightly poke food with a fork so hot air can escape from inside the food.

Scrape – Use a rubber spatula to clean food out of a bowl or container.

Set – When a liquid becomes more solid as it cooks or cools.

Sprinkle – Scatter an ingredient lightly over top of something.

Stir - Mix with a spoon.

Tender – Food that is cooked until it's soft enough to cut and chew easily, but is not mushy.

Thawed –When a frozen food item warms up enough so that it's no longer frozen.

Undrained – Keep the liquid in which a food has been cooked or stored.

Whisk – Mix in a circular motion using a whisk.

Index

About the Author

Phyllis Pellman Good is a *New York Times* bestselling author whose books have sold nearly 10 million copies. Among her bestselling cookbooks are **Fix-It and Forget-It Cookbook, Revised and Updated: 700 Great Slow-Cooker Recipes**, and the other *Fix-It and Forget-It* books in the series. The recipes in **Fix-It and Forget-It Kids Cookbook** are drawn from those books.

Good's first cookbook for children was *Amish Cooking for Kids: For 6- to 12-Year-Old Cooks*, which she authored with her daughters, Kate Good and Rebecca Good.

For a complete listing of books by Phyllis Pellman Good, as well as excerpts and reviews, visit www.Fix-ItandForget-It.com or www. GoodBooks.com.

If you've enjoyed this book, you may want to explore our other cookbooks with hundreds of delicious, easy-to-make recipes—

⇨ *For slow cookers:*

Fix-It and Forget-It
Cookbook
Revised and Updated

Fix-It and Forget-It
Christmas
Cookbook

Fix-It and Forget-It
5-Ingredient Favorites

Fix-It and Forget-It
Lightly

Fix-It and Forget-It
Diabetic Cookbook

⇨ *For stove-top and oven:*

Fix-It and Enjoy-It!
Healthy Cookbook

Fix-It and Enjoy-It!
Diabetic Cookbook

Fix-It and Enjoy-It!
5-Ingredient Recipes

Fix-It and Enjoy-It!
Cookbook

*New York Times
bestselling author
Phyllis Pellman Good*

National Bestsellers!
Nearly 10 million copies already sold!

My Cookbook Diary

I made this recipe	Date when I made the recipe	How the recipe turned out
....	....	....
....	....	....
....	....	....
....	....	....
....	....	....
....	....	....
....	....	....
....	....	....
....	....	....
....	....	....
....	....	....
....	....	....
....	....	....
....	....	....
....	....	....
....	....	....
....	....	....